He Guides My Path

SARAH BERTHELSON

He Guides My Path
by Sarah Berthelson

Printed in the United States of America

Library of Congress Control Number: 2002113883
ISBN 1-591602-84-X

Xulon Press
11350 Random Hills Road
Suite 800
Fairfax, VA 22030
(703) 279-6511
XulonPress.com

To order additional copies, call 1-866-909-BOOK (2665).

This book is lovingly dedicated to
my husband George for his
encouragement, support and editing
and to
my sons, Chad and Shay,
who are blessings
beyond measure.

Contents

CHAPTER ONE

God Sent Me

"Train up a child in the way he should go and when he is old, he will not depart from it."
—PROVERBS 22:6

On a cold winter morning I came into this world, weighing a fragile five pounds. The first few months of my life were hectic for my parents, Ruth Summers and Lemmie Reid, as I needed constant care in that I developed pneumonia shortly after birth and I had an ear infection that the doctor thought would leave me deaf. Neither of these problems was more than temporary in nature. I was born in my Grandfather Summers' farmhouse in Lincoln County, Mississippi. This house my parents shared with him while farming his land, since he was almost ninety years old when I was born.

The Lord had already blessed my parents with two sons, George Dewey and Wiley, and two daughters, Mary and Billie. This gave my parents the family they had dreamed of, two boys and two girls. Then I came along. I messed up their plan but not God's.

We lived near Brookhaven, a lovely small town that anyone would be proud to call home. I am thankful that I was raised in this environment. It made me appreciate the blessings that God sent into my life through the years.

The last child born into a southern family usually acquires the nickname "Baby". My family always called me "Baby" unless I had been bad and then it was "Sarah Ruth". I knew if Daddy called me by my name that I was in trouble. This nickname was a bit embarrassing during my teenage years. Later I grew accustomed to it and in fact, I enjoyed the special title.

My parents were the most fun loving parents a girl could have. They were delighted when my friends came to our house and they laughed or cried when I did. My Mama was the disciplinarian with me. She didn't hesitate to cut a switch from the nearest bush and use it on me when she felt it was necessary. This happened more often than I care to remember. Mama was also my best friend and I could share my happiness or troubles and heartaches with her. She often quoted Bible verses to me to make a point clear. I felt fortunate to be sent into this home. I was like most kids and pouted with my mama if she didn't go along with my desires. That got me absolutely nowhere with her. She just let me pout, never giving into my ugly behavior. I learned that pouting did no good for getting my way. I eventually gave up that trait.

If measured against acquired status symbols, my family would have been termed poor beings. We did not own a car or even own our own home but it never occurred to me that we were poor because we were happy. My family worked hard on the farm and we had plenty of food to eat and clothes to wear. Sometimes my clothes were hand-me-downs from my sisters or cousins but I also received my share of new clothes so I never felt cheated. I had two aunts that could sew, Aunt Lou and Aunt Jessie, and they made many of my clothes. I never felt deprived. No matter what we lacked in material possessions, our home overflowed with love for each other. It was important to my Mama that we loved each other and upheld each other. My sisters and brothers were always close. When one of us needed someone, we looked to each other. That is the way it is in a Christ centered home.

I cannot remember when I didn't love Jesus. His name was honored and respected in our home. My parents taught me that Jesus loved me at a very early age. They saw to it that I went to Sunday school and church. To accomplish this, we had to walk about one and a half miles to catch a school bus that Mr. Versie Nations owned and he would take us to church. The walk to and from the bus was fun and a time for chatting and laughing. Going to church was the highlight of my week. My friends that attended school with me also went to my church. It seemed to me that the entire community was one big happy family and I felt that all my friends had happy and secure homes just like I did. Even my High School principal, Mr. L. L. Simmons, was a dedicated man of God and a deacon in our church. As such, he had a tremendous influence on my life. At this point in time, my life was so secure and non-treating that I had no fears.

At age eleven I became aware of the sin in my life. I knew I needed Jesus as my savior as stated in John 3:1-8, "Ye must be born again". This was to occur during a revival in our church. I still remember the feeling I had as I walked the aisle to make my decision, to follow Christ as friends sang 'Oh Why Not Tonight?' a favorite old hymn of mine to this day. What a joy it was! That very moment I knew the Holy Spirit had come into my life and would be with me throughout my life here on this earth. In addition to all this I also had the blessed assurance of eternal life with Christ. God would guide my path.

There is a river not far from our church in which I was baptized, Fair River, along with all the others that had made a profession of faith during the revival. I think about twenty-five people were baptized that day. I can still see that picture of all those people wading into the water. *"One Lord, one faith and one baptism"* Ephesians 4:6. Following my baptism, something unusual happened to me, as I was changing my wet clothes, I noticed a small minnow (fish) fall out of one sock. Even at that young age I remember thinking, I will be a fisher of men for God.

"And He saith unto them, follow me, and I will make you fishers of men".
—MATTHEW 4:19.

Jesus guided my path as I continued to grow physically and spiritually. As a young girl of twelve, I often read my Bible to my parents. We talked about the Bible and Mama would share with me the knowledge shared with her by her father, my grandfather Summers. At this time in my life I still thought that all children grew up in homes just like mine.

Even in childhood I was aware of the sins in my life. There were times when I yielded to temptation and I knew when I had disappointed God. When there was sin in my life, I felt irritable and unhappy and my days were not filled with Christ's joy and peace. During these times I would often take my frustrations out on the ones I loved. I learned from my bad experiences, that to be happy, I had to be in the right relationship with God. I had to pray without ceasing. God was always there and ready to forgive me. What a loving heavenly Father! There continued to be times when I was not willing to ask forgiveness and once again I would lose that sweet peace and joy that comes only through God's forgiveness of sin. *"For thou, Lord, art good and ready to forgive: and plenteous in mercy unto all them that call upon thee."* Psalm 86:5

About a week before Christmas, Mama would

start her Christmas baking and all the delicious pies and cakes were placed in a cupboard. As I reflect on my memories, I can remember one incident where temptation was too much for me. Mama had made this lovely cake and placed colorful jellybeans all over the top of it. Every day I would go to the cupboard and take one or maybe two jellybeans, until they were all gone. It never occurred to me if I took one or two that soon all would be gone. Well the day arrived when my Aunt and her family from Louisiana came to visit us and Mama went to the cupboard to get her lovely cake, except it wasn't so lovely anymore. I will never understand how she knew that I was the one who ate the jellybeans. I am thankful God gave me parents who disciplined me. *"Train up a child in the way he should go and when he is old, he will not depart from it."* Proverbs 22:6. A tiny little switch on my legs taught me that I was not to take things without asking my mother, not even a sweet jellybean. I do not recommend whipping or beating on children but I do believe in a swat now and then. Our children are the losers when they are not disciplined. God certainly disciplines His children. Why should we not love ours children as much?

God guided my path through elementary and

junior high school. I could best be described as an average student who loved people. I cannot recall anyone at our school that I did not like. Oh there were times that I would have a disagreement with a friend, and would not like that friend temporarily but soon my anger was lost in my love for that individual. God had given me the ability to forgive. My classmates did not use drugs or alcohol and hence I did not face that problem. Young people today have more things to tempt them than I did. The worst thing my friends and I could think to do was to smoke a cigarette but I would not dare because I knew for sure my Mama would find out. I was always amazed that my mother could find out the bad things I did before I could make it home. Moms are like that. When I went away to college and had freedom to make choices, I would not go to places that some of the other kids went because of my mother. I often thought of how disappointed she would be in me if I went to places that a Christian should not go. I thought of how Mama would feel more than I thought about God in many of my decisions. Maybe that is not so bad. More children need to respect their parents as I was taught to respect mine.

I loved sports but wasn't good at any of them. I

was active in the 4-H Club and Y-Teens but I lacked self-confidence in all areas of my life. I was not a mature Christian and felt very insecure. I felt that everyone was prettier than I was. I compensated for these feelings of inadequacy by being silly or funny. Playing pranks on my friends and making people laugh was a joy to me. My pranks were not at other people's expense because I never wanted to hurt anyone, since it was painful for me to see a friend unhappy. Because of this, I exhibited an outgoing behavior and was voted the wittiest girl in high school one year. A surprise to me in that I had to find out from Mama what it meant. It meant that I was the silliest one they could think of. Oh well, we have to have something to look back on to be proud of. I at least made the contest.

Daddy drove the school bus that I rode and this made me very happy. It was a joy to share my Daddy this way with others and all the children at school loved him. I didn't mind Daddy loving them, but I do remember feeling a bit jealous if Daddy gave any one child special attention.

As I entered ninth grade, we moved from the 'old place', as it is now affectionately called, to our new home, the only home ever owned by my parents. This move was made possible after my oldest brother, Dewey, started working for the Public Service in New Orleans and was able to purchase a two-bedroom frame house with twenty acres of land and gave it to our parents, until their death. This was a wonderful thing for Mama, Daddy and I. By now, my brothers and sisters were grown and were making a life for themselves; therefore I was the proud occupant of my very own bedroom. The house was soon enlarged with ample room for all the family to come and visit.

We still lived in the same school district so I continued my High School education at Fair Oak Springs. We now lived much farther away from Fair River Baptist Church where I had spent fourteen years of my life and we felt God leading us to one closer to our house. Wellman Baptist Church is where my teenage years would be spent. Dewey had purchased a car and left it with us, so I learned to drive. I have often thought what a great man my brother Dewey was. He was one of the most unselfish people I have ever known. If he had a dollar then the rest of his family had one. He was so generous. He saw a need for our parents and met that need. Because of his job and generosity, we had a nice home and transportation. Godly men are generous men. He was more concerned about meeting the needs of his aging parents than he was of having money and things of his own. What a wonderful way to remember my oldest brother.

My life, like every other person's, certainly has not been without problems. One of the memories that I reflect on is when my brother Wiley and I were playing by our old barn and I saw this huge wasp nest. Those are things country kids are use to seeing. I was afraid of the wasps but my big brother told me if I would lie down and play like I was dead, they would not sting me. So here I am lying on the grass when he takes a long stick and hits the nest. He ran for all he was worth. There were at least seven of those things that did not care if I was dead or alive. They stung me! My dear daddy, who did not smoke or chew tobacco, found some tobacco somewhere and he chewed the tobacco and placed it on my stings. I learned that day, you don't play dead just because your brother tells you to. Common sense is still the best indicator of what we should do in a crisis.

School days have changed since I was a student. I honored my teachers as my parents had taught me. I knew that if I got into trouble at school, my parents would not take my side. I was taught to respect older people, people in authority, our leaders and my country. I still say "yes sir" and "yes mam" to people that are older than I am. I am appalled at our young people today that do not respect their teachers or parents. I am qualified to say this since I am a teacher and a parent. I pray for our students today in this world that is so different than it was when I grew up. Prayer changes things; parents we need to pray.

I was so happy to be growing up. I loved my family, my school and my church and all the people that I knew. We did not have a television or a telephone until I was in High School. Now, I realize that was such a blessing. I used my imagination to play. I remember cutting up the Sears and Roebuck catalog and made paper dolls. My goodness, I had everything a girl could wish for. I had a playhouse that I marked off on the ground with a stick. It was a three-bedroom house and the sticks and jar tops that I used as silver wear and dishes were as good as anything one can buy at the store today. Our children are God given gifts but they have more than enough to play with. Most of their rooms look like a toy store. Have we failed them by not letting them use their imagination? God guided me and was there all the time in my growing up years. Today I thank him for his presence in my life at that time of my life. God bless our children as they are exposed to so much in this day and protect them so they will not stray. I pray for the parents that they will take them to church so they can feel your presence and know you are their Savior just for the asking.

"Train up a child in the way he should go and when he is old he will not depart from it."
—PROVERBS 22: 6

CHAPTER TWO

God Are You Calling Me?

"As ye have therefore received Christ Jesus the Lord, so walk ye in him."

—COLOSSIANS 2:6

I always felt God was calling me into a special service for Him. At church I would do anything I was asked to do and one Sunday I even sang with a men's quartet. This was really being bold, as I am not one bit musical. God took care of that situation by giving the men strong voices so I could not be heard. They needed an extra voice and I was flattered to be asked, very nervous but flattered.

At the age of sixteen I dedicated my life to full time Christian service. There was this feeling inside me that God wanted me to serve Him on a daily basis, maybe to be a missionary. I said to God that day that I was willing to become what he wanted me to be. After that important decision I was still far from perfect. I often thought Christians should be perfect and wondered why I couldn't achieve this perfection. I often felt ashamed and ugly for the sins in my life. I am so thankful now for those feelings of guilt. God loves the imperfect.

I never hear preachers today ask for young people to come forward to dedicate themselves to full time Christian service. I heard one pastor say that if you are a Christian you are in full time service but that is not the way I see it. There is something about walking down the aisle and saying to God and the people "I am going to serve God faithfully all the time". Sometimes when I was asked to serve in a position I didn't particularly care for, I would think of that commitment and then I would do it. Many times I served in Vacation Bible School because I would remember my promise and then receive such a blessing for serving him in that area.

As a youth I can remember how unworthy I felt of God's grace. It is so easy for young people to fall into the sinful traps of the world when they do not remain close to God on a daily basis. God wants us to be our own person. He made us unique individuals. He made us in His image. *"So God created man in his own image, in the image of God created he him"* Genesis 1:27a. I am a sinner saved by grace. Often I had thought that I would have to break one of the Ten Commandments to sin and since I knew I didn't, I would feel all pious and wonderful about myself. It is these thoughts and attitudes that would get me in big trouble. When I think of the fruits of the Spirit, "Love, joy, peace, longsuffering, gentleness, goodness, faith, meekness, and self-control", there are many days that I do not pass this test with even an above-average grade. How about you?

I have added an incident in each chapter that shows while I was attempting to do God's will, I was still a typical sinner saved by grace. One incident was my senior year of High School when some friends and I decided to take a ride and go to Percy Quinn State Park in McComb, Mississippi instead of attending school that day. One of our classmates was wealthy enough to own his car, so we got off the school buses and got into Dan Furr's car. We were going down the highway, happy as could be, and Dan decided to pass this slow moving car. Well I looked at that car and there were my mother and brother Dewey going to McComb to the eye doctor.

Nothing I could do but wave and so did they. When I arrived home that afternoon my mother said, where have you been? OK, I was caught again and had to fess up about my one and only day of playing hooky from school. I have never understood how my mama was so smart and devious enough to get an eye appointment on the same day that my classmates and I decided to go on a picnic.

"I also will laugh at your calamity; I will mock when your fear cometh."
—PROVERBS 1:26

After graduation from High School I wanted to go to college. I went to Copiah-Lincoln Junior College, which was only nine miles from my hometown of Brookhaven. The day I arrived at Co-Lin, I was so frightened, I could not think straight. I had no idea what to do or where to go. It seemed like all I did for two days was stand in lines. It only took a couple hours before I had met new friends. God had given me a Christian roommate. My parents were not financially secure and could not afford to pay for my education, so my sister, Mary, paid my first semester tuition. She asked me to let her do this for me. I felt very fortunate to have a sister that would help me to get an education although I felt badly that she had to work hard and give me her money. One day at Co-Lin, the reading teacher called for me to come to her office where she gave me an eye test. I knew that I had lazy-eye-blindness but I hadn't told anyone at school. The teacher said to me that I was eligible for a rehabilitation scholarship from the state. I never had to pay another cent on my tuition or books. My handicap was now an advantage. God blessed a blind eye and I was able to get my degree from the University of Southern Mississippi. God was there all the time. God can take our disabilities and make them work for his good. He did that for me.

College life was exciting. I became active in the Baptist Student Union organization (BSU). I attended an early morning, prayer group called 'Morning Watch'. This was a great way to begin my days at college. I began to grow as a person and to have more confidence in myself. I gave devotions and I even led in prayer at the BSU meetings. I even found that I was not afraid to share Christ with my friends.

One day the BSU Director came to my dormitory room and explained the Student Summer Mission Program to me. She asked if I would consider filling out an application to be a Student Summer Missionary that summer. She explained my chances were not good since I was only a freshman and the requirements were for students that had completed their sophomore year. I thought I would please her and fill out the application but I did not expect to be going anywhere. A few months passed and our BSU planned a trip to another college for the BSU State Convention where the Student Summer Missionaries were to be announced. It was such a thrill to hear my name called. I had to go on the stage to say a few words and I was so scared my knees were shaking. The theme of the convention was 'May the Lord Depend on You?'. I closed my few words by saying the Lord could depend on me as I was going to Oklahoma City in His service that summer.

Being the baby of the family and having never been away from Mississippi, I began to have doubts of going away but I did not share these doubts with anyone. The excitement of being a Student Summer Missionary began to vanish from me. Three weeks before I was to leave for the mission field, I became ill at college and had to have an appendectomy. As I lay in the hospital, I began to think of the wonderful excuse I had not to go to Oklahoma City. I could tell everyone I wasn't physically able to make the trip and they would only feel sympathy for me. Before I could bring myself to tell my family or friends of my decision, I remembered that commitment I had made to God two years earlier, 'I will go where you want me to go, dear Lord'. I prayed about going to do this mission for him and began planning on the clothes and other stuff I would need to take with me. Certainly I was nervous and scared but I knew that God was going with me. It is always a comfort to know that wherever I go, he is there guiding me through my days and nights.

My six weeks in Oklahoma were spiritually rewarding. I worked in Vacation Bible Schools, took census for area churches and shared my testimony in revivals. I had many unforgettable experiences; one was the night I saw a sixteen-year-old girl give her heart to Jesus after I had witnessed to her earlier that day. God was with me as I served Him in Oklahoma. I received some wonderful training by serving in Vacation Bible Schools where I was the superintendent and had to do a lot of speaking. It was the first time that I had witnessed for my Lord Jesus on a one-to-one basis with young people. It was also the first time that I saw the rewards of witnessing for our Lord Jesus. During this period, more than a dozen children and young people accepted the Lord Jesus as their savior. This was a blessing indeed to see that God blessed this work for him and I will never forget that wonderful summer.

As I returned to college my sophomore year, I was still confused about my future and what God wanted me to do with my life. I had a genuine love for children so teaching seemed to be the career in which to prepare for and thus Elementary Education became my major course of study. In the second grade I had loved my teacher, Mrs. Allen, and I wanted to be just like her. She was kind and helpful and never once do I remember her being anything but a sweet lady.

Upon completion of my sophomore year at Co-Lin, I went to New Orleans to get a job for the summer. My sister, Billie, had asked me to come and live with her in order to save my money. I went to the telephone company and filled out an application for a job about 9 a.m. The phone rang at Billies' about noon and this lady told me to be at work at 1 p.m. Another miracle had taken place in my life-I had a summer job! The boss of the Directory Department just happened to be from Brookhaven and my sister, Mary, worked with his sister. Now doesn't God work things out just perfectly?

After working two weeks, I received my first check. This was the first time in my life that I had money I had earned and could spend anyway that I wanted. It was sixty dollars, I believe. As I continued working and receiving my checks, I began to think how nice it would be to advance with the company and make even more money. The idea of having money seemed more exciting than going on to college. The more I thought about making my decision of quitting college known to my family, the more I thought of the commitment I had made to God. I resigned my position with the telephone company two weeks before the fall quarter began at Mississippi Southern. I had made some wonderful friends at the telephone company and I knew I would miss them. It had been a wonderful experience and it gave me confidence because I knew now I could work if I needed to.

Senior College was quite different from Junior College. With hundreds of students more and much more freedom, I had to decide for myself how I would spend these last two years of college. I became active in BSU, where I met many new and wonderful Christian friends. During my time at Southern, I attended Main Street Baptist Church. This was a good outlet in that I could get away from college and mingle with the families that lived in town. I had gone there to make a speech about my mission trip when I was a sophomore at Co-Lin, and was placed in a home of two lovely elderly people, Mr. and Mrs. McKinsey who became like family to me. When I arrived at senior college, I already knew someone. I would go home with them after church and spend the afternoon, then go back to church and then ride the bus back to campus.

As I completed my college education I prayed for God's guidance in finding a teaching position. My roommate and I signed contracts the same day to go to Meridian, Mississippi as fifth grade teachers. It was a thrill to call my parents and share with them my plans of going to Meridian to teach. They were not as excited as I had hoped, after all Meridian was 120 miles away from them.

College was an exciting time for me. I worked at having friends and letting them know that I cared about them and their concerns. I was not the best student in the world but I did my work and I had a lot of fun also. Dormitory life was a blast. I had to keep my room clean and learn to share my small dormitory space with another girl. I was blessed with the roommates I had. I never asked for any certain girl but I always ended up with a wonderful

Christian roommate. There was a bond between each one that I lived with.

I did some very crazy things at college. We had a BSU retreat one-week end and as we were walking across this huge river bridge, one of the students dared me to jump in. Without one single thought, I bailed off the bridge into the river, not once thinking of the consequences. I went deep down into the water and seemed as if I would never rise to the top. Needless to say, I did because I am writing this book. Three days later I had the worse earache that anyone could endure. I went to the doctor and found that I had burst my eardrum. To this day, I am still having problems with that ear. After thinking about that incident through the years I have realized we need to have patience with young people. They go through some stages like I did that are really weird. As I grew into my young adult life I have often thought how quickly I could have died. I had no idea if there was a tree or anything else in that river when I jumped. I now think of all that could have happened to me that day but peer pressure has always been a factor in growing up and that day I just responded to the moment.

I am thankful that I grew up before the drugs, the sexual revolution and all the other stuff that our young people today are bombarded with. When young people make a mistake and come to me for advice I try not to judge them because I remember the stupid things that I did as a youth. As an adult we should not forget that we were young once. Were you perfect? I am so thankful that God protected me through my youth and that mama never found out that I jumped off the bridge.

"Forsake the foolish and live and go in the way of understanding."

—PROVERBS 9:6

CHAPTER THREE

Thank God
for Anna

*"I am crucified with Christ: never the less I
live: yet not I, but Christ liveth in me: and the
life which I now live in the flesh I live by faith
of the Son of God, who loved me and gave
Himself for me."*

—GALATIANS 2:20

My roommate, Marolyn, had gotten a beautiful Plymouth for graduation from college. I
felt I had gotten one to, since my friend took me
anywhere I needed to go. I was fortunate that we
taught in the same school because transportation
was not a problem for me. I longed for a car of my
own, but did not see how I could afford one my first

year of teaching since my monthly check was only one hundred and eighty dollars. Things have sure changed a lot.

Teaching was such a rewarding experience for me. Every boy or girl that came into my classroom was special to me. I sincerely felt God had made it possible for us to meet. I loved the children and was deeply concerned about their spiritual needs.

Calvary Baptist Church was the church God led me to attend during this year. Brother Otis Seal was my Pastor. He meant a great deal to me and was always there when I needed a friend to share my burdens with. He was eager to pray and share God's Word with me.

I led my fifth graders in a time of devotion daily and they had the opportunity to go outside the room if they did not want to listen to God's Word. I never had a student to go outside and not listen to the devotion. They looked forward to that time as much as I did. We pledged allegiance to the flag and marched to the Marine Corps Hymn. I was young and had a great time with my students.

One day after the bell had rung for recess, a little girl, I'll call her Anna, came up to my desk and asked how she could become a Christian. First I thought I would choke before a word came out. I was stunned;

you see Anna was a Jew. I knew the difficulty Anna would face with her family if she became a Christian. My first thought was why Anna, Lord? This was not going to be easy. Anna did not see how shaken I was. I soon relaxed and caught Anna by the hand and said, "I'll show you how". About this time the bell rang and the other children returned to the room. I immediately gave them some 'busy work'. Anna and I went into the cloakroom where we sat on the floor and I began to find scriptures and read them to her (John 3:16, 10:10b, 14:6, 1:12; Romans 3:32, 6:23, 5:8 and Revelation 3:20). After reading these scriptures I asked Anna if she wanted to pray and ask Jesus to come into her life. She did and that was the sweetest prayer I had ever heard. With that prayer, her entire attitude changed.

One day her mother came to school to say thanks to me for the change in her daughter. I asked if I could give Anna a Bible. Anna was so proud of that little white book that contained the words of Jesus. This was the highlight of my teaching career. Her mother was gracious and even allowed Anna to go to a revival with me. My pastor talked to her in private and she told him how the Lord Jesus had saved her. I learned through that experience that if God sends someone to you, not to fear, He would be there to guide you.

Calvary supported a little mission across the railroad tracks in Meridian. The people met in a very dull building with no pulpit furniture or pews. The windows on this building even had bars on them. It looked more like a jail than a place of worship. The people's needs were great since they were poor people. The children did not have good clothes to wear to an up-town church. There was a desperate need for a church in this area.

One day, Brother Seal asked me if I would go and work in this mission. Many of my friends thought I was crazy. I loved the people there and the work was rewarding. God blessed that little mission. Often the Pastor was late for the eleven o'clock service. He pastored two small churches. The other church had their worship service at 10 o'clock, and then he would drive several miles to preach at our mission at 11 o'clock. I taught the adult Sunday School class and when Sunday School was over, I would lead congregational singing until the Pastor arrived. This was certainly a surprise to everyone that knew me, since I cannot sing very well. Several Sundays, I would be giving a devotional thought when the Pastor came in and he would just nod for me to continue. In this mission, I received some good training in all areas of church work. I was just having fun serving him there, not realizing that he was growing me for other services.

One of my dreams was to brighten the church up with some pulpit furniture and some pews. I wasn't making enough money as a teacher to do much. My tithe was only eighteen dollars a month.

I was on my way to school one day in my brand new car which I had purchased two months earlier, singing a Christian song like I always did on the way to school, when suddenly there was a loud bang. A truck, owned by a gas company, just turned across the lane in front of me and we crashed. It totaled my car and crushed the cartilage in my throat. Needless to say I didn't talk for a while. I got a settlement from the insurance company and praise the Lord; I was able to purchase the pulpit furniture for the mission. Isn't it amazing how God can turn something that we think is so bad in to something wonderful for him?

"And we know that all things work together for good to them that love God, to them who are called according to His purpose."
—ROMANS 8:28

God watched over my life daily as I served Him

in Meridian. There were many times I failed Him and did not seek His will in making decisions. Each time I left Him out of my decision-making I would feel that I had made a mistake. One that stands out in my mind was an impulsive buying spree. Several girlfriends and I were riding around town one Saturday morning and spotted a beautiful car on a car dealer's lot. It was a dream car as far as I was concerned and without much thought and no prayer, I asked my girlfriend to stop. There was a salesman waiting to sell me that flashy car. I never really enjoyed owning that car; it was more of a burden than a pleasure. I did learn to seek God's guidance from then on in the things I purchased.

Living in an apartment with friends taught me to get along with people. Working with people in the mission taught me to have a deeper love for all people. God's love is a forgiving love. Being closely involved with people, I learned to forgive. Many weekends and holidays, I would spend with my family in Brookhaven and my friends enjoyed going home with me. My family welcomed my friends as part of our family. My parents were a joy to be around and made everyone feel like part of the family. That is the way all of God's children should behave. I soon found out that not all people had a loving family like mine. Some of my friends did not dare ask me to go home with them. The attitude of their parents would not have been kind since it would have been a nuisance to have a visitor messing up their plans.

One of my deepest fears was the fact that one day God would take my parents to be with Him. In my mind I could not accept this fact, that one day our happy family circle would be broken on earth through death.

Every Saturday morning I would call home to talk with my parents. It seemed that sometimes there could be misunderstandings between my friends and me but my Mama always understood me. She was the wisest lady that I have known in my lifetime. She knew exactly what to say when I had a problem and it was always a godly answer. She taught me so much in how to live my life for Jesus. It concerns me today that so many parents are too busy to listen to their children or when they might listen, they have nothing to say. I never once felt that my problems were not important. If they were important to me, they were important to my mother. I still live by her advice in many ways and I hear her words come out of my mouth often.

CHAPTER FOUR

God Sends
My Mate

*"Call unto me and I will answer thee and show
you great and mighty things which you knoweth
not"*

—JEREMIAH 33:3

A t about age sixteen I prayed daily that God
would choose my mate and I would know him
to be God's choice when I met him. As I was growing up and noticing the boys, my heart would often
flutter when a special smile or wink came my way.
These boys were very special and were my first
loves. The boys I grew up with taught me that boys
were kind, affectionate, happy or sad and that they
were truly good people.

College brought new boy friends into my life and a new awareness of what kind of person I would like to fall in love with. A very special friend came into my life and after a few dates, he told me that he loved me. I began to think about what the word 'love' meant to me and realized it was a word that should not be tossed around lightly. I decided then to not say, "I love you" to a male friend without meaning it with all of my heart. I did not want to say these special words just to get to wear a boy's class ring, like I saw so many girls do. Even though it put you in another status category if you had a boys ring, I didn't want to do that.

I became confused about this young man's feelings. How could he say he loved me if I didn't love him? I went to the BSU office to talk to the director. I learned a lesson that day that was very meaningful to me throughout my courtships. The young man that had fallen in love with me, or said he had, was not a Christian. The Director said to me "never date anyone you would not want to marry, for you never know who you will fall in love with". I thought about that statement often in the days after. I dated young men that did not have the characteristics of the person I wanted to marry but I knew it was possible for me to fall in love with them. I had some big crushes on a boy or two, but in my heart I knew they were not that special one from God.

There were several special friends that came into my life. I often thought, "This is the one" but not enough to say, "I love you". I knew I had to be very sure before I used those words.

Being a single teacher was fun. Many of the parents of the children I taught, plus other teachers and friends were constantly finding a date for me. It seemed the idea was to get me married. I had dreamed of marriage as I grew up visualizing the prince charming that would come into my life. In my mind, he would be a Christian, preferably a Baptist, a college graduate and be settled in a job so we could have a nice home. If possible, he would like to live near Brookhaven, so I could go home often to visit my family. I definitely had a very selfish vision of my man to be.

One Saturday in Meridian, my roommate and I were busy with the usual Saturday chores, such as washing hair and cleaning the apartment when the phone rang. It was a young man calling my roommate from the local Naval Air Station, he wanted to come to see her and bring a friend. I was not thinking of my life's partner at the moment, therefore, I did not take the curlers out of my hair. I would never let a date see me in hair curlers but this wasn't a date. They came over and I was introduced to George, a Marine Aviation Cadet from Montana and in pilot training. We were cordial to each other but no lights were flashing or bells ringing. In fact I did not realize he had even noticed me until he called a few days later and asked me out. George was a Christian and attended the Christian Church. He too had prayed for his mate while growing up. George was not from a Christian family, yet I had never met anyone that loved the Lord more.

My family was often critical of some of my dates. It seemed I could not date anyone that all members of my family approved of. This was one of the prices I paid for being 'the baby' of the family. George visited my family during the Thanksgiving holidays and to my amazement, all gave him the stamp of approval. It was a bit frightening to think that I had found my special someone. I prayed daily about my feelings for George. We prayed for each other. George did not want to make a mistake anymore than I did because we planned on marriage being forever. This guy seemed a little unreal to me since he had prayed for the same type person that I had prayed for, a partner that would be devoted to him until death separated them.

Dating is an exciting time of one's life. I believe that since marriages are made in heaven, we have to seek God's leadership in choosing our mate. I wanted to be in love with several young men before I met George but there was always something lacking. George and I shared the oneness that could only be made complete in God. I was surprised to find out that I was in love with a guy that did not fit into the mold that I had dreamed up. He was a long way from being a Mississippian, the career he had chosen was frightening to me, as I do not like to fly, and we certainly couldn't settle down in a home of our own for at least twenty years. And of all things, I did not dream of being a military wife but God knew that together we would be missionaries for him all over the country.

When George asked me to marry him, he said, "we cannot tell anyone until I receive my Aviator Wings". It was against the rules for a Cadet to marry while in pilot training. I was willing to wait but he wasn't. His reason for not wanting to wait was he did not think I would wait for him. What a joke that was to me, I was smitten!

Four months after we met, we were married in my parent's living room with my family present. I could not get married without them being there; my family had always been very close. My preacher brother, Wiley, preformed the simple ceremony.

George was sent to Pensacola, Florida almost immediately, then to Kingsville, Texas. We were married in February and he received his wings in November of that year, a long time to keep such a wonderful secret. God guided our path to Havelock, N.C. where we started our service for Him by finding a church to serve in.

My husband is a godly man and he is the leader of our home. God is first in his life and this has made our life together such a joy. Every night he has a devotion with me and prays out loud. It doesn't matter where we are, on vacation or at a relative's house; he gets out God's word, reads to me and then prays. What a joy to have the head of my home, seeking God's leadership in all that he does. I thank God for the day that he sent this wonderful man into my life to be my mate for life. Our young people need to make it a matter of prayer for their mate. Parents should pray the moment their child comes into this world for their mate. God answers prayer, not in the way I think he should, not in the way I thought he would, but he answered them in the best way for me. I am so thankful that he didn't answer all my prayers in the way I desired. I would have certainly married someone other than my George.

Keeping a marriage a secret is not as easy as it may sound. Like most young ladies, I had dreamed of the white wedding gown, floating down the aisle on Daddy's arm but that didn't happen. I was married is a beige suit, the only thing I could afford. Having my family there at our secret wedding just was not enough for me. I had to go to Canton, Mississippi and tell my former roommate. When I got back to Meridian I then decided I needed to tell my pastor. Telling this secret wasn't over for me because now I thought "I need to tell my principal". Needless to say this made my new husband very nervous. I wore my wedding ring on a chain around my neck and thought it was a cool thing to do. It was really exciting when I was asked out on a date by some of George's' buddies after he had left Meridian. Of course I never went out with anyone because I was married and knew it. He was not thrilled about the asking but I enjoyed it because of our secret.

After George complete his training in Pensacola, Florida, he was sent to Kingsville, Texas to finish his training and to be commissioned. When school was out he found an apartment for me and I went to Texas to be with him. The first Sunday I was there, I went to Sunday school but not with George since he had flown to California on a required cross-country flight. The room was full of young adults. The group was asked to introduce themselves, so I proudly said, "I am Sarah Berthelson". That was not a smart thing for me to do as one of the guys said to me, "I checked your husband in a few weeks ago". Oh boy had I messes up or what? Since he wasn't supposed to be married, I thought for sure I would get him kicked out of flight training. The nice young man did not tell on us.

"The Lord is on my side I will not fear what man can do unto me."

—PSALM 118:6

CHAPTER FIVE

A Child Is Given

"For my thoughts are not your thoughts, neither are your ways my ways saith the Lord. For as the heavens are higher than the earth, so are my ways higher than your ways, and my thoughts than your thoughts."

—ISAIAH 55:8,9

George and I love children and from the moment we were married we dreamed of the day we could have a child. Due to a surgery I had when I was eighteen years old, my doctor told me that I would probably never be able to conceive and bear a child. He warned me that I should tell the young man that I would marry that I may not be able to have children. The hardest thing I had to do when George asked me to marry him was to tell him I might not be able to have a child. He simply said, "That is ok, if God wants us to have a child we will have one". We did not lose our hope.

After our first year of marriage this dreaded thought that I would never conceive became a reality. I went to several doctors from Mississippi to North Carolina and they all said the same thing, "maybe you should think of adoption".

This was the first time in my life I experienced real bitterness toward God. I was so ashamed of these feelings but I had them. I questioned Him, "Why God won't you give me a baby? All my friends are having babies, why can't I?" After all I thought I was a pretty good person, teaching Sunday School, reading my Bible and praying every day. All these questions and thoughts brought me to self-pity. Finally, one night I could take the agony and frustration no longer. I had become miserable and had made George miserable too. We sat down and had a long talk and took a deep look at ourselves. George said, "I think we need to pray". We went into our bedroom, knelt beside the bed and gave this problem to God, "Lord if it is your will give us a child, or if it is not your will, make us content in your choice for us." What a peace I found in my life in the days to come. I was calm within; the storm that had taken over my mind had settled. I took one day at a time trying very hard to please God with my everyday life.

I became content teaching my Intermediate Girls in Sunday School. When the church needed a Girls Auxiliary leader, I began to work with these girls. Even the sixth grade class I was teaching at school became more important to me. Most of all this busy schedule of mine was no longer a chore; it was a great joy!

Several months passed and I became very ill. The doctor told me I was pregnant. Oh, what a thrill for George and me as we began to make plans for our life with our child. The time passed and it was time for my pre-natal checkup. It felt as if a bomb had shattered my dreams when the doctor looked at me and said, "I am so sorry to tell you this but you are not pregnant, you have an ovarian cyst and it should be removed immediately". I don't remember the drive home. I cried so hard and wondered again "Why Lord, why am I going through all this heartache?"

George made reservations for me to fly to Brookhaven the next day, to be near my family for the surgery. He drove to Mississippi after making arrangements for military leave from his unit.

This ordeal was almost like loosing a baby. My mind was convinced that I wasn't going to be a mother. I knew I had to read my Bible and pray often so I would not be overcome by the depression that followed the surgery. I stayed with my parents a month for recuperation, and then returned to Havelock where I resumed all my duties at school and church.

Another year had passed when George and I decided we would go to an adoption agency and see if we would qualify for a baby. We went through this long grueling procedure over the course of a year and finally our home was 'set-up'. The agent told us all we had to do now was to wait for a baby to come available. Once again the prospect of finally becoming parents overwhelmed us with joy.

As we were anxiously waiting for that precious moment to arrive when the adoption agency would call and say our baby had been born, another disruption occurred. George came home from work one afternoon and said "Honey, I have orders. We are going to Camp Lejeune, North Carolina". That wasn't so bad since we were only moving fifty miles and figured we could just continue with the adoption. Wrong again, we were changing counties and would have to go through the adoption process in that county. We thought we could just have our adoption agency transfer our paperwork to the new county and wait for the baby to arrive. We soon found out that this is not the way agencies worked. Since we had moved to another county, we had to go through the entire procedure all over again but in this county there was a two-year backlog of applicants and no social workers. By this time we just completely gave up on the idea of adoption since George would only be there one year before moving again.

We were at Camp Lejeune about three months when George was deployed to Guantanamo Bay, Cuba for three months of duty. I could not see staying there by myself so I packed up my belongings and went to Mississippi to stay with my parents.

I was outside washing my dad's car on a hot summer day as my parents sat on the porch and watched, when the phone rang. I ran inside to answer it and that phone call changed my life. It was from my sister, Billie, who worked for the Telephone Company in New Orleans. It seems that the day before, while on coffee break, several ladies were discussing their children when Billie said to one of the women, "I wish my sister and brother-in-law could have a child. They want one so bad and they would make wonderful parents." As the ladies began to leave the lounge, one lady stayed behind to talk to Billie. She told Billie that her landlady's niece, in a far-away state was pregnant and they were going to put her in an unwed-mothers home in a couple of weeks. This lady asked Billie if she could mention George and me to the landlady. Well Billie had a phone number for me to call in this far-away state, so I could talk to this young lady. I called that number and this sweet, child-like voice answered. I explained to her who I was and she said she knew. She said she would be happy to come to Mississippi and live with my parents and to let George and me adopt the baby. After talking to her I thought "Oh how can I do this without talking to George?" I knew there was no way I could call him in Cuba. As I was out on the porch sharing the conversation that had just taken place, with my parents, the phone rang. It was George calling from Cuba! He was on one of those two-way radio/phone patches and all he could understand me to say was "a baby" and "a plane ticket" during all of the 'over and outs' of that type conversation. I finally made him understand that I wanted him to call me on a regular telephone. My parents were on an eight-party-line telephone system and all the community would be able to pick up and hear the news, so I went to my sister Mary's house in Brookhaven. George called me there within twenty minutes.

Plans were made and the ticket was wired to this young lady. In just a few days she would arrive in Jackson, Ms. All I knew was what the color of dress she would be wearing and that's about all she knew about me. I knew she had to be a very brave and special person to consider this proposition that I had offered her.

"And whatsoever ye shall ask in my name, that will I do, that my Father may be glorified in the Son."

—JOHN 14:13

As the plane cleared the runway and taxied toward the terminal, I thought my heart would stop. I was wondering what she was like and what my baby would be like. Soon I saw this beautiful, sixteen-year-old young lady, with a red dress, walking down the ramp. "There she is", I said to my sister, Mary. "She is so pretty." As she came closer to us, she looked up with those tired and frightened eyes and said "Sarah". "Yes" I said to her as we embraced. She became a part of our family for the next few months. We loved her and she loved us. She called my parents MaMa Reid and PawPaw, just as the other grandchildren did. I could not have asked for a sweeter friend than what she turned out to be. My brother, Wiley, and I led her to the Lord one evening and she was baptized in our little church. She said to me, "I have a new life now and I am giving you one." She would always refer to the fetus as my (Sarah's) baby.

Our son, Ky, was born and given to us through adoption. He was the most beautiful baby I had ever seen. When he was placed in my arms, I cried for joy and thanked God for this miracle of birth. My family was now complete!

When Ky was eight months old, I went to the doctor for a check-up and he told me I was pregnant. I said, "I'm sorry but I can't get pregnant. I have a son by adoption". He replied, "I am sorry too but you are pregnant". I left his office confused and not at all excited. I told George what the doctor had said. He wasn't at all excited either. We did not think much more about my diagnosis until a couple of weeks passed and I began to get very ill every morning. When I went to see my doctor, all he had to say was "I told you, you are pregnant." Seven months passed and I gave birth to another beautiful baby boy, Chad. I already knew that I loved Ky more than I had ever thought it possible to love another human being but when they placed Chad on my chest, I was totally ecstatic. Giving birth was a wonderful experience and I was so proud of this beautiful baby and loved him immediately. Ky was fifteen months old when Chad was born. It was almost like having twins. They sure kept me busy.

I had one major problem in that George was sent to Vietnam two months before Chad was born. Before he left, he moved Ky and me back to Brookhaven to be near my family. I had my moments of depression, worrying about George, and feeling pangs of self-pity; just knowing he would not be around for the birth of our second child. Chad arrived in God's timing. He was a handsome toddler, very energetic, happy and such a joy to my family and me. My parents came to visit us daily.

The war was bad and I listened to the news daily and would be so scared when I heard of a plane crash or any mention of an attack on the base where George was stationed. Life was bearable only through a lot of prayer. I knew God heard my prayers for George and I knew George was praying for us. Chad was a week old when George called from the Philippines to see about Ky and me. I was still in the hospital so my mother was the one who gave him the wonderful news of the birth of Chad.

As a military wife, I soon learned I could not always depend on my husband to be around for special occasions such as birthdays, anniversaries, and having babies.

Chad was eleven months old when he first saw his dad. Things had changed a lot in our household since he left. With two active baby boys, I had become a very busy mother, having little time left for myself and even less for George. We went to Pensacola, Florida for George to serve as an instructor for pilots in training. We became active in the youth work at our church. It seemed that there were not enough hours in the day anymore. Yet, this was one of the happiest tours of duty I had experienced. Being a mom and taking care of our little boys was the greatest.

George was busy being a flight instructor and I was busy being a housewife and mother. I began to feel the responsibility of parenting was all on my shoulders and I resented it. George had changed; he wasn't as helpful and loving as he was before he went to Vietnam. I had to tell him to take up time with the boys. All my time was taken up washing dishes, cleaning house, feeding kids, washing clothes, teaching good manners, wiping tears, etc. I could go on and on but you have all been there. The statement, never a dull moment, really applied to me. I was the busiest woman in the world and my life was never boring or dull but the joy had suddenly gone out of mothering. At the end of each long day, I was exhausted and wanted nothing more than a hot bath and to go to bed. On the other hand, George had been flying all day, so he wanted to go to a movie or just take a ride around Pensacola. I knew he had no idea of what my day had been like or did he seem to care. I felt he did not appreciate me for keeping his children and his home in ship-shape condition. Our relationship was not the same as it was before he left for Vietnam. We would set for hours and not talk to each other. What had happened to the two people that were so much in love and wanted their lives to be happy and fulfilled? I'm sure that many busy housewives can relate to this.

The only way we could recover from this drab life was to put God first in our home. I had to realize that my boys were not to take the place of God or George in my life. We began to read our Bible and pray together again. I got some help two mornings a week to clean the house and sit with the boys while I would go visit a friend or go shopping. Now I had an outlet. It was now a joy to see George pull into the driveway at the end of the day. We were romantic again. Our lives were centered on God and the joy was there. He guided us through some very difficult times.

"He that sayeth he abideth in Him ought himself also to walk as he walketh."

—I JOHN 2:16

After three years together in Pensacola as a complete family, my world caved in, as I would once again hear my husband say those awful words, "Honey I am going back to Vietnam". I felt I could not face another separation with George going off to fight a war. I cried for days, making my life and all my family's lives miserable. Then came the acceptance, as I knew my Lord would not leave me nor forsake me.

Plans started to fall into place. Here we were going back to Brookhaven; the place I kept running back to when I needed security. We bought a house in a wonderful neighborhood with very little traffic and a big yard for the boys. I know God chose this house for me. It was the perfect place for us, plus there were a dozen children for our boys to play with.

George had to go to the Los Angeles area for a month of refresher training in the F-4 aircraft he would be flying while stationed overseas. Not wanting to be away from each other any longer than we possible had to, he bought a camper and took the boys and me with him for the month. We did a lot of sightseeing, going to Disneyland and all the wonderful places families can enjoy in that area. There was only one problem I was sick. I hated to complain and upset George about my health. He was sorry to leave us and he didn't need my problems. I thought it was just nerves about the impending separation and I would be fine once we got settled in our little house.

The day prior to George leaving for Vietnam, he took me to our family doctor, Dr. Wilkins, who had delivered Ky and Chad. The diagnosis, "Sarah, you are pregnant". I cried! There was nothing else I could do, since I would be having another baby without my husband being there. It seemed almost impossible that this was happening but such was the life of a military wife.

Shay, our third son, was three months old when

he met his Dad. Shay was a beautiful baby and brought much joy to us. He was fun to play with. Ky was now in Kindergarten and Chad was four. My family helped with the children to get them to church. Shay was such a blessing and more than I ever expected God to do for me. My boys were my motivation to get me going in the morning, just to be there meeting their needs and loving them. God had answered our prayers by giving us a family. I had wanted a girl but not getting one did not change a thing. My boys were the center of my life and everything I did revolved around them. I loved being their mother and taking care of them. It was not always easy but it was always a joy.

I still think of the times that my blessings were babies and then in their toddler years. Ky was the one that was fascinated by pots-and-pans and took them out of the cabinet daily. I think it was a challenge to him to see how fast his mom could put them back so he could take them out again. Chad came in this world with an engineer's brain. He took toys, clock or anything he could reach apart and then attempted to put them back together again. It was fascinating to watch him at play but it was not easy for me to put his things away, piece by piece. Shay was my child that was not afraid of anything. He was drawn to water regardless of where it was. One of the funny things that happened with Shay at about one year of age was when the phone rang one morning while I was rushing to get to a Bible Study. I opened the top to the washing machine for the washer to stop while I answered the phone. To my shock when I came back into the kitchen, Shay had climbed onto the table, crawled across the top of the washing machine and was standing happily in the washer full of water and clothes in his pretty go-to-church clothes. I am thankful I never missed a moment with my boys and have so many wonderful memories of them. My sons taught me that they came into this world with their own personalities and curiosities. I knew that I had to nurture them in their own abilities and love them unconditionally in their personalities. Oh what a blessing it was to me, to have the family that God had planned for me. I believe in miracles, I have three!

"For I was my father's son tender and only beloved in the sight of my mother."
—PROVERBS 4:3

CHAPTER SIX

A Great Adjustment

"Verily, verily, I say unto you, He that hearth my word, and believeth on him that sent me, hath everlasting life, and shall not come into condemnation; but is passed from death unto life."

—JOHN 5:24

When George came home from Vietnam, we went to Beaufort, S.C. I was happy with this duty station and we became members of Laurel Bay Baptist Church. The Sunday we joined the church, the Pastor was leaving for a new church field. Still we felt God leading us to this church and there were numerous opportunities to serve Him there.

George was soon elected Chairman of the Deacons, which was a full-time job in a church without a pastor. We even found ourselves being called upon as counselors for all types of problems. Through this we realized not all homes are happy homes and we even had to deal with couples who broke up their marriages. We spent many hours in prayer and counseling with our friends. We often wondered why God had put us in this position. This was all new to us and we prayed more than ever. We knew we could not help these people if we did not let God speak through us. The only way He could do that was for us to lean on Him daily.

I was elected Director of the Sunday School, another position that was very demanding. It was such a joy to serve in this area of church work. I never even thought about the shy person within me or that I did not have any confidence in myself. I knew that through Christ I could do this job, if that's what He wanted me to do. It wasn't easy and the devil was active there. One of the greatest pressures I encountered, was the fact that some people did not feel a woman should hold this position in the church. I knew the Lord had led me there and I would not give up because of these pressures. It was a blessing to serve him and to learn from this position.

I remember thinking at this time that God was preparing me for greater service in the future. I did not know what that service might be but I did know I felt his presence in my life in a very real way.

After our church called a pastor, my burdens and George's were lighter. New areas of service continued to open in our lives. One day the pastor asked if I'd teach a study course for the Pastors and Sunday school Directors of the Association. This was to teach every night for a week. My first impulse was to say "no and you have to be kidding" but then I told him I'd pray about it. I have never been more excited about teaching a study course and it turned out to be one of the highlights of my stay in South Carolina. These men, the class only had men in it, were so kind and attentive to this young lady and her ideas. Well they really weren't my ideas since I got them from a book.

All things were wonderful and we were completely happy until one day I felt burdened. When these feelings would come over me, I always wanted to go home to see my parents. I called George up and asked him if he could take a week of leave. He said "sure but what about Ky and Chad being in School?" "We'll just take them out for a week." This was very unlike me to allow my children to take off from school.

We went to visit Mama and Daddy and had a wonderful time, relaxing and talking. Daddy was happy as ever and thoroughly enjoyed the boys. He took them for walks to the pond and he gave them rides on his bicycle. He had the best time with these three little grandsons that he was so proud of. After all, they belonged to his baby.

Our week was up and we went back to South Carolina. Within an hour after our arrival, Mary, my sister, called to tell me that Daddy had a heart attack. It was serious and for me to come home. On the plane from Savannah to Jackson, Mississippi, I was stunned. I cried and could not think of words to say to God. I wanted so much to have my parents around me forever. Was my daddy going to die? Oh how I wanted God to heal him. Somehow I knew it was time for Daddy to leave us. Daddy lived about three months but he was hospitalized most of this time. It gave me a chance to tell him how much I loved him. I know God guided my path and sent me home to have that week with my Daddy. That is just the way God takes care of his children. He doesn't leave anything out.

After Daddy's funeral, we went back to South

Carolina. Once we were home, things happened to me physically and mentally that I could not understand. A friend that had lost her mother told me I was in a stage of grief. She gave me a Christian book about grief and I began to recognize my symptoms.

I went to the school and signed up to substitute. It was an outlet and I taught 2 or 3 times weekly. This gave me an opportunity to do one of the things I enjoy most – teaching children. The children helped to take my mind off the grief that I felt. Ky and Chad were in school but Shay was only two. I found this wonderful lady that said, she would come to my house every day and take care of him. Shay loved her and they would go to birthday parties and play at the park. He was perfectly content with his friend. It was good for him and it was good for me to get out and take my mind off my grief.

Mama did not adjust well to Daddy's death. I talked to her weekly by phone. She was sad because half of her had died. On November 9th, only five months after Daddy 's death, I was teaching when George and one of my girl-friends came to school to inform me that Mama had died. She was standing, getting a chest x-ray in the hospital and had a heart attack. I could not believe what I was hearing.

We flew to Mississippi that evening to be there for her funeral. My best friend had gone to be with God. I could not face my feelings. I was sad, angry, and very frustrated. Only God could calm me. He understood how I felt. I cried and prayed for Him to help me. He did. As I look back on those unhappy days I know now I could not have faced them without God. What a peace He brought to me. Oh I will always miss those sweet parents but I am assured of meeting them again in heaven. I often thank God for giving me to Ruth and Lemmie Reid. They were exactly the parents that I needed.

Death of loved ones come to all families. It's something that cannot be explained to anyone. One has to experience it to feel sympathy for others in times like this. I've experienced it and now God is using it!

I enjoyed my parents telling me about their life as a child and young person. It amazes me that that most of us can't imagine our parents every being children. My dad lived on a huge farm where his dad had six hundred acres of land in Lawrence County, Mississippi. There were twelve children in the family and all were expected to work hard on the farm. Each of his siblings was born in the farmhouse. Daddy really never knew exactly how old he was because my grandfather would give each boy a few acres of land when he turned twenty-one and Daddy always thought that grandpa kept him twenty for several years. He rode a horse to court my mother. I often think of how hard it had to be compared to this day when we have so many modern conveniences. They had to wash their clothes in a big pot and get their baths in an old cold tub. I thank God that I was born during the washing machine days.

My mother was raised on a farm and had eleven siblings also. I suppose in those days that the parents had these big families to help with the chores. My grandparents were devoted to the Lord Jesus Christ and it showed in the family that they raised. Most of the children grew up to be dedicated active Christians. She shared with me about quartet groups and camp meetings where they went to worship. She had wonderful memories of growing up in a Christian home and she passed her Christian beliefs on to her children.

"She is more precious than rubies and all the things thou canst desire are not to be compared unto her"

—Proverbs 3:15

CHAPTER SEVEN

A Needed Rest

*"For this God is our God forever and ever. He
will be our guide even unto death."*
—PSALMS 48:14

S oon after the death of my parents, George
received orders to Millington, Tennessee. As
much as I loved Laurel Bay Church and my
Christian friends, I welcomed a change of pace in
my life. As a true military wife I was ready to move
on. This lady, that had once wanted to settle down in
one spot and live there, now had the military blood
and was anticipating the move. Through this I could
see how God could change a persons dreams and
make life even better than we can imagine.

I was physically and spiritually exhausted. We

Christians do not like to admit the fact that we can get this tired serving our Lord. This was real and it happens often when we are too busy with church and family. I was not on a mountaintop; I was in a valley with my Christian life, needing to rest, get refueled and renewed. It took this time of rest for me to begin to grow again. It took me a long time to see how God can work in this type of situation. Remember He never leaves us nor forsakes us. We are the ones that turn our backs on Him and say look Lord I need to do this my way.

Being caught up in all the activities of the Church and at school, I had no time left to be alone with God. I was too busy to be effective. I learned though this that young parents need to slow down sometimes, even in our church work. It seemed as if I lived at church. The boys were in their mission activities, boy scouts, school, and sports. Now as I look back they were too busy. Children need some down time and some playtime that is not scheduled for them. We made mistakes and now I realize I kept my children and myself too busy.

We had lived in government quarters for years and I dreamed of a home away from the base and just maybe one in the country. Yes God gave me that quiet place to live when we arrived in

Millington. In fact it was twelve miles from the base. It was a lovely new home with a room for each boy and plenty of room for the children to play.

God led us to Brighten Baptist Church in Brighton, Tennessee. A sweet-sweet spirit was in that place. It was one of the warmest and sweetest fellowships I had experienced. The pastor, Brother Pat, came to visit us soon after our arrival. I shared with him how I felt that God had placed me there to be fed on His word and to rest. I wondered if he didn't think I was a lazy Christian and just did not want to do anything in the church. He understood as I shared with him my emotional state; he allowed me to rest.

We attended Church regularly, had wonderful Christian fellowship and I did not take on a lot of responsibility. I attended a ladies Sunday School class and grew spiritually. God showed me what I needed to be taught by a wonderful lady, Mrs. Elizabeth Simonton, that became my close friend. After a year in a class I felt led to teach the seventh through ninth grade girls in Sunday School. This was fun and not at all exhausting. It was like a breath of fresh air to be with these precious young ladies.

One of my dreams had been to go to Ridgecrest Baptist Assembly in North Carolina. The church made it possible for my family to go. They paid our expenses. It was truly a mountain top experience for all of us. I learned new teachings methods to be used later. In fact I learned more about the work in Sunday School than I had thought possible. I wondered what God had in store for me next. I had begun to expect greater things from God as he had used all of our experiences for Him.

We spent two glorious years at Brighton. What was next? Our future turned out to be more than I ever could have dreamed of. George received orders to Iwakuni, Japan. He had expected overseas orders and we knew that he was to go alone; meaning that the boys and I would be without him for another year.

The boys and I began to make plans to move back to Brookhaven. I had not prayed about it and asked God's guidance in this matter. I took it for granted that this is where we were to go. We went to Brookhaven to find a house. We soon realized there was none available that was large enough for the boys and me or they were too expensive. God closed that door.

Dr. Stover from Texas came to Brighton to lead

us in revival. I went to every service. It was so inspiring and I felt Gods presence in such a real way. On Saturday night when the invitation was given, George slipped past me, went down the aisle and dedicated his life to Christ to be used for Him in Iwakuni, Japan. Tears rolled down my cheeks as Bro. Pat told the congregation the decision George had made. He had not discussed this with me but I knew how dedicated he was and how he wanted his life to count for Christ in his military service.

The next few days of my life were miserable. I didn't like anybody or anything; I could not understand the bitterness that seemed to have taken control of my life. What was happening to me? My life was so miserable and my husband seemed so content. Once again I had left God out and I was doing things my way. Oh why couldn't I learn this lesson of giving my days to Christ? I went into my bedroom, closed the door, knelt down by my bed and gave this problem to God, even though I wasn't sure what the problem was. I asked God to show me what He wanted me to do with my life while George was away. I was willing to let Him take control. I had really made a mess of things on my own.

A couple of days passed and I realized I was at peace with myself and with God. No more bitterness or frustration, I was calm. Then I had this strong desire to accompany George to Japan, even if it meant we would have to pay our own way and for me to home school our sons. Had I gone completely out of my mind? No way had I ever had a desire to go to another country. Why was I thinking like this?

As I was sitting in the den I picked up a Brotherhood magazine and began to thumb through it when I noticed a page about Lay Missionaries. It told of how people were needed to work with Career Missionaries overseas and at home. I got up and called the Foreign Mission Board. A nice lady excitedly told me about this ministry and would send me material. God is this what you are trying to tell me? Could I really go with George and serve you there? When George walked through the door for lunch, I kissed him hello and said, "I'm going with you to Iwakuni". He looked startled as I shared with him my call to the Foreign Mission Board for details.

The Board sent pamphlets and information concerning Missions in Japan. They sent the addresses of missionaries that I could write. One problem was we did not have any missionaries in Iwakuni, Japan. The Foreign Mission Board suggested that we start a Sunday School in our home. We were going to be missionaries on a Foreign Field. How exciting!

We gave our testimonies at church and shared our excitement with our beloved church family. We even had a commissioning service. This service was one of the highlights of my Christian experiences. Our three sons, George and I pledged to God and our church that we would serve Him in Japan. My dear brother, Wiley, came and preached the commissioning service and that made it even more special.

We purchased our airline tickets, got our passports and visas. It seemed we were on our way to Iwakuni, Japan.

We went to Ridgecrest with our friends from church. It seemed that God made a way for us to go there. After a week at Ridgecrest and only a few weeks left before we were to leave, George received a call from the base to tell him that his orders had been changed. He wasn't going to Iwakuni; he was going to Okinawa. Our first impulse was to panic. Instead we knelt down by our bed and gave it to God. Within three days the tickets and everything else was in order for us to go to Okinawa. The big difference this time was there was no time to contact the missionaries on Okinawa. We went on faith, knowing God would have us a home and a place to serve.

Brighton was a happy place for all of us. Most people will never forget our family because of some of the antics of the boys. Ky or Chad decided to toss a rock one night at church and it went right through the window glass of one of our dear ladies. The reason I said "or" is that we never did know who did what. Each boy would always point at the other and would say he did it, regardless of what they did. The lady was gracious and George had her window fixed. When Shay was 5, our pastor was going to show slides of Vacation Bible School but he kept getting the slides upside down. Shay who was sitting in the back of the church with his parents, lets out this yell and said, "Brother Pat, you don't know what you are doing". After that the VBS slides were not so important since all in the church were laughing their heads off, that is except for Shay's embarrassed family.

"Even a child is known by his doings whether his work be pure and whether it be right."
                    —PROVERBS 20:11

CHAPTER EIGHT

A Foreign Land

"Teach me to do thy will; for Thou art my god: Thy spirit is good; lead me into the land of uprightness"

—PSALM 143:10

We left Jackson, Mississippi on August 17, 1977 and we were just a little afraid of the unknown situations ahead of us. Knowing we had no place to live and we were not sure our children could go to the American school on the military base. We also worried about what kind of medical facilities that were going to be available to us. Many unanswered questions and thoughts flowed through our heads.

Shay was six years old and did not understand the

full meaning of the trip. He wasn't at all excited about flying on the airplane. He kept asking if daddy could fly the plane if the pilot became sleepy. His dad assured him that he could.

Ky and Chad seemed excited about their adventure but I am sure uncertain thoughts bounced in and out of their minds also. Both were fine Christian boys and they felt God's presence in a very real way in their lives. They talked often of how they could witness for God on Okinawa.

George just seemed happy to have his family going with him. The times he had been overseas before were only bad memories of separation.

My concept of the miles from Mississippi to Japan was inaccurate. The longer the plane was in the air, the more I wondered how much farther it is to Tokyo. We were in the air about 18 hours before landing in Tokyo.

The first glimpse of the Tokyo International Airport was astounding. There were hundreds of people standing in lines trying to board planes or get through customs. Right away I recognized there was a language barrier; I could not hear one southern drawl.

Being very tired and wanting to find the hotel we were to stay in, we began to find our way around

the airport. It seemed that there was always someone close by who could speak some English. Soon
we were sent to a waiting room where a limousine
would pick us up and take us to the Hotel.

Tokyo at night is breathtaking. I had never seen
such a great city with as many tall buildings. A very
tired family of five soon arrived at the Plaza Hotel, a
very modern hotel. It was much more than I had
expected. The airline was paying our expenses at the
hotel since we could not make flight connections
that night to Okinawa. Ky and Chad shared a nice
room with two double beds while George, Shay and
I were in another room with two more double beds.
We could not wait to get a warm bath and fall into
those beds.

About 2 a.m. I awoke to the sound of Shay
breathing abnormally. He was having an attack of
asthma. We had no medication so George went
downstairs to the desk clerk to get directions to a
drug store. George could not speak Japanese and
the young man could not speak English. On top of
that, the drug stores were closed. We prayed for
Shay and he was soon comfortable enough to sleep.

The following morning we took a short walk near
the hotel and I got my first look at the city by day. It
was hard to believe the buildings could be built so

close together. We were to leave at 2 p.m. to go to the airport for our flight to Okinawa. After standing in line at the airport for about two hours, we were informed our flight would not leave until 8 a.m. the next day and back to the hotel we went for another night. We were disappointed that we had wasted the day and did not have an opportunity to take a tour of the city.

The bus arrived at the hotel about 7. There weren't any more limousines for us. At last we boarded the plane for the little island that was going to be our home for one year. Our mission field was just a few hours away.

We arrived at Naha, Okinawa about 2 p.m. and took a taxi to the base so George could check in. Upon arriving at the gate to the base the taxi pulled over for us to get out. We didn't want out. We were about a mile from the building we were to go to but the taxi did not have a base sticker; therefore, it could not get on base.

Here we are standing on the side of the street when a gentleman stopped and asked if he could help us. He took us to the required building, then called a military vehicle to come and take us to the transient quarters where we would stay until we found a house in the village.

After getting settled into the transient quarters. George called the Baptist Missionaries to share with them our excitement of being in Okinawa to serve as Lay Missionaries. We were invited to an English-speaking church for the services the next morning. Our luggage did not arrive when we did, so we did not have a change of clothes. We washed the clothes we had worn on the plane so we would be clean for church.

We visited all three English-speaking churches on the island and prayed for God's leadership in finding a church home. We were led to join Central Baptist Church. Reverend Bud Spencer, his wife Doris and son Jonathan had returned to the island one month before our arrival. They had been in the States on furlough.

While Brother Bud was stateside on furlough, the church had many problems and the Sunday School attendance was down to 56. After arriving on the island and finding the church in such a sorry status, Bro. Bud and Doris had prayed that God would send them someone to help build the congregation up. They prayed this prayer at the same time that George's orders were changed from Iwakuni to Okinawa. Isn't God great!

They were very strong Christians with a deep,

genuine love for all the Okinawan people. They had been on the mission field for 16 years. They were burdened for souls to be saved and that unchurched people would find a place to worship. I felt God's leadership in making a decision to work with the Spencers.

We got up early Monday morning eagerly anticipating finding a house to live in. After going to several apartments and even more houses over the next few days, our excitement was gone; the apartments were so small and expensive. The houses were expensive and unfurnished; we had no furniture. I began to think there wasn't a place for us. I even doubted God's leadership in my decision to be there. We prayed for God's guidance in finding a place to live.

The next day George rented a car and we saw an ad for an apartment we thought we should check out, even though it sounded very small and way too expensive. It was a clean, Japanese style, furnished apartment with only 500 square feet of living space and rented for 80,000 yen which was $300.00 per month plus utilities. It got even more expensive as the exchange rate of the dollar declined. We rented the apartment! Our bedroom had a bed in it. The boys shared a room and they learned what futons are. From our third story apartment we could observe the Okinawan people as they went about their daily activities in the village.

We had to move into a temporary apartment, in the same apartment complex, for ten days before our apartment was available. The day after we moved into our permanent place, George was sent to the Philippians for two weeks of school. I didn't understand why he had to leave us so soon. We did not have a car and I knew very few people. God was preparing me for an adventure that I could have never dreamed of.

The Spencers picked us up for Church services and for everything else taxis became our mode of transportation. God showed me quickly that I was to lean on Him and not George for this duty He had called me to.

The boys walked a mile to a school bus stop to attend different schools on Kadena Air Base; Ky was in the seventh grade, Chad attended fifth grade and Shay started the first grade. This was a blessing for them to be allowed to attend these American schools and even more of a blessing for me since I didn't have to home-school them. The first week of school, each boy missed the bus at one time or the other and I would call a taxi to take him to school.

They got accustomed to riding in the taxi alone.

Then to top off all my confusion in trying to adjust to this new culture, there were typhoon warnings. I didn't know what a typhoon was, but I soon found out. My Japanese friends later told me that the typhoon had not hit the island but I was not convinced. I had never been in such wind and rain in all my life. Living on the third floor didn't help my situation either since I could hear the winds more than if I had been on a lower floor.

George came home for one week then was sent back to the Philippines for another week. About this time, I was feeling that George's orders should have said Philippines instead of Okinawa. Our children learned to play with the Japanese children although they did not speak a word of their language. It was amazing to see them play together, understanding what they were to do next and to laugh. They enjoyed going into the neighborhood papasan stores, the Okinawan neighborhood convenience store.

One of the very few farmers in our village could speak about twelve words of English. He enjoyed the boys and the boys loved him. He became a good friend to me as well. He and I could communicate by me pantomiming to him. He could understand me by my gestures. We were invited to his home on several occasions. It was an education to sit with his family on their floor and have tea. Papasan, as we called him, became our dearest Japanese friend.

In the meantime Brother Bud was busy getting thing organized at Central Baptist Church. He appointed a steering committee to nominate people to fill various positions. The church needed a Sunday School Director and there was only one person in the church who had experience and that was me. I was elected by the church to serve in this capacity. My experience from serving God in South Carolina was paying off. As Sunday School Director, I worked hard at organizing all areas of our Sunday School. George served as the Men's teacher.

My job was very demanding, as most of my teachers were military men and their wives. We worked hard and the Sunday School began to grow. God blessed our church but most of all He blessed me. I felt His presence in a way that I had never felt it before. I was not afraid when George had to leave me for weeks at a time. George spent most of the year being a carpenter. He fixed the Spencer's Lottie Moon house and did numerous repairs and electrical work at the church. Would you believe he grew up as a carpenter's son? He had gained a lot of knowledge growing up helping his father and now was using it working for our Heavenly Father. I took care of our boys in all areas of their life, school and church activities.

Everyday on the Island I realized how great it is to be an American and to know Jesus Christ as Savior and Lord. So often I had taken these things for granted and would forget that I was bought with a price that Jesus paid for me on Calvary.

As I look back on this year that God gave me, I have nothing but fond memories. There were hard times, sad times, lonely times, and times of sickness but not one time did I feel fearful. God went to Okinawa with me and was there to teach me through all the experiences. He knew what was best for my family and me.

I must add that there were many funny things that we remember. Shay the youngest only knew one word in Japanese and it meant 'stupid'. Now isn't that just like a six-year old? He decided to use his one word on a playground one Sunday afternoon. The next thing we learned was that the older brother of the child that had been wronged would beat up on the older brother of the aggressor, which was Chad in this case. Chad was the largest in size of our boys so the big brother of the Japanese child attacked him. Chad had a sweet spirit and did not care to fight but he was hit anyway. Ky thought it was funny that this happened since in actuality he was the oldest son. I did not see the humor in it. Shay was chastised for using his one and only Japanese word.

I was not going to drive on the island. I announced this to my husband but he thought I should take the driver's test anyway since he was going to be gone a lot. I reluctantly took the test. After taking the test and as we were leaving the testing center I asked George "What does POV mean?" What a laugh he had since it meant 'Private Owned Vehicle' and I had no clue they were even talking about a car. Regardless of my lack of this important knowledge, I passed the test and George bought a small car for me. I enjoyed having it for church and running back and forth to school. I soon learned my way around the island. I was not the best driver and all the streets were very narrow. I sideswiped a light pole one-day as it was pouring down rain. Chad came home from school and said "Mama, you have a big stick sticking out the side of the car." It turned out to be part of the pole I had hit. God is so good to his children and meets our needs even when we are stubborn and do not want them met.

Family life in Okinawa was much like a single parent family as George was gone so much. I spent a great deal of time going back and forth to the school. Each boy was in a different school from the other two. Chad was a very mischievous fifth grader. He was very smart and did his work quickly but I did not say that he did it well. That was his problem with his teacher who thought he should be doing so much better academically. She called me in often to tell me of his lack of interest in his studies. What is a mother to do? We had a lot of talks and I became very frustrated with him for keeping his teacher upset. I believe that a child does not need to be a bookworm or a straight A student. That was a plus for my boys, since each one had plenty of potential academically. Ky was the quiet one in Okinawa and his problem was that he did not care about making friends. He knew he was going to be there one year and gone. He and his brothers had a close relationship so that was enough for him socially plus the children at church. Shay was the one who got to know the Okinawa children and enjoyed playing with them. They didn't know what the other was saying but to Shay playing was enough. I learned to say hello in Japanese and to bow when I passed them. That was just being courteous.

CHAPTER NINE

Retirement and Raising Our Sons

"I am crucified with Christ; nevertheless I live: yet not I but Christ liveth in me, and the life that I now live in the flesh I live by the faith of the Son of God."

—GALATIANS 2:20

My happiest years were those spent raising our sons. What a joy they were to my life. We had fun together as I taught them about our Lord Jesus. They were good boys and each gave his heart to the Lord at a young age. They grew in Him through Church and all the activities that it had to offer.

Chad was entering high school; Ky was starting

the eleventh grade and Shay the fifth grade when George retired from the Marine Corps. They were typical boys and continued to be the highlight of our lives; our world revolved around them. They were smart and did their work at school like normal kids. I substituted at their schools to keep my eye on them and to be near them. They enjoyed their growing up years.

We were loving parents and wanted them to have every thing that we didn't have as we were growing up. When they turned sixteen, along came the cars. They wore nice clothes and went to a private school. There were things that we did for them that we really couldn't afford but we just wanted them to be happy, well-adjusted young men.

Ky was only seventeen when he graduated from high school. He seemed like he was still my baby as we moved him into his college dorm. I remember looking back at him as we drove away and the look on his face as he watched us drive away. Oh, how my heart sinks when I remember that moment.

College life was typical for him. He was a good student and wanted to please his friends and family. This was not easy since we were the old way-of-life and college was so different. He was introduced to a freedom that he did not know how to deal with.

He was partying with his new friends and still trying to be the boy he knew that his parents desired him to be. He began to change. We found out that he was smoking pot and doing things we did not approve of. This was hard to admit since I still thought of him as my perfect boy. We went through some difficult times with his rebellion. He didn't understand himself any more than his family did. I cried many tears trying to get him back into church and to being the son that I knew.

One night he came home with a bottle of liquor and went to his room. Shay saw him and told his dad and me. George went to his door and asked him to open it and he reluctantly opened the door. I was sitting in the den when he came downstairs crying, and put his head in my lap like a little child; I was crying too. He said, "Mom I need help, I do not know what is wrong with me." I asked him if he would go for counseling and he said he would.

The next day I got an appointment for him. After testing, the doctor told us he was bipolar (manic-depressive). I didn't know what it was but knew that I had a friend who suffered from this mental illness and I couldn't believe that my baby was facing this same problem. He was so intelligent and artistic, how could he have a mental illness?

Through the next several years, we lived with him being very high or very low emotionally. When he was depressed he would not talk to us or do anything but stay in his room. He would argue about any and every thing. As a family, we did not know what to do for him or say to him. None of us wanted to argue with him. He was very sad.

Chad graduated from high school and went on to college. He was a good student and did well there. His future wife, whom he knew from high school, went to the same college. Their college years were typical and both graduated with a Master Degree. Chad is now an Environmental Engineer. God brought him back to Memphis after 10 years of working in Florida. What a blessing to have him and his family near us again. By now his family had grown beyond him and Brenda to include a son Parker and daughters, Summer and Heather. I can see God's hand on this dear family as they serve him and as they raise our grandchildren to love and serve our Lord Jesus.

Shay was home with us for four years after his brothers left the nest. We enjoyed him and he was so much fun. Shay went to college and is now married with a lovely family consisting of his wife Melissa, a son, Chase, and two daughters, Hannah and Hope. It is God's grace that we have our children close by. Shay calls and checks on me often and I know I can depend on him for any need. He and his family are active in a local church serving our Lord. What more could a mother ask. How thankful I am for my godly family.

I skipped the details of Shay and Chad's college years. Their lives were typical of all college students, always needing money. Academically and socially they did fine. They had learned from the pain inflicted by their brother's rebellion and never took us back down that road.

Ky ultimately dropped out of college and worked in many jobs. Typical of a person with bipolar disease, he would go into work and quit his job but with his charm and good looks, he would have another job within hours of walking away from the last one. He called me almost every day. We were close and he needed his parents. His brothers continued loving him with all their hearts. As a family we tried very hard to please him and help him in every way possible.

He started back to college after moving back home and was doing great; he even made the President's List. He only had a few hours to go until he would receive his degree. When he came home from college one afternoon, I had his favorite lunch ready for him, a taco salad. He ate and we talked and laughed. He was working on an assignment for school that required the typing of a paper, so he went to his room to work on that.

Later that afternoon, he went about a mile from our house and committed suicide. When the sheriff came to tell George and me, I thought I would die. I have never been so hurt in my life. I had lost my dad, my mother, my nephew and now my son. "God how can I go on?"

I blamed myself for not seeing the signs and I felt that I had failed him in some way. He was my baby and I loved him. I knew him so well, why couldn't I see his pain? I questioned myself as a mother. Where did I fail my son?

My heart goes out to love ones that have to go make funeral arrangements. It is very hard to pick out a casket and do the things that have to be done. I was so numb that I just went through the motions and there are things that I now wish I had done differently. But at that time I could not think and just wanted to get that part of my pain over with.

When Ky was very young he had told me he wanted to be buried by my mother, his wonderful Mama Reid. That rang in my ears as I thought about the funeral arrangements. My mother was buried in Brookhaven, Mississippi but I wanted the funeral to be in Millington, Tennessee where our friends and church family lived.

My family and I did what we needed to do. My extended family was there for us. Christian friends and family reached out in love and concern. In my heart I knew that my savior knew my pain. I do not know how anyone can go through the loss of a loved one without knowing our Lord Jesus. He loves us so and he softens the blows. I knew that He loved Ky even more than I did and that's a whole lot of love. If you don't know my Jesus, stop right here and pray for Christ to come into your life and live in you. Ask forgiveness of your sins and live for him. Go to church next Sunday and find a family of God that will love you through your difficult times. Find your ministry that he will lead you to do for him. He is so near, please don't push him away.

Don't Cry

The tears were flowing down my cheek
When someone said, mom may I speak
Of course, my child, as I tried to sound spry
Oh, my dear mom, don't cry, I heard with a
   sigh

I choked back the tears and I tried to smile
As the beautiful bride walked down the aisle
It wasn't the wedding that was making me cry
It was the loss of a son that would not be
   there.
My youngest son was looking for his bride to
   come to be his wife
With the happiness I had in my heart
There was the bride who would fill an empty
   hole that was in my soul
I couldn't forget the one that was missing
   today
If he could have spoken about the hurt in my
   heart
He too, would have said, "mom, don't cry
Look at the spark in my brother's eye"

CHAPTER TEN

Grief–Oh What Pain!

*"Fear thou not for I am with thee; be not dis-
mayed for I am thy God; I will strengthen thee;
yea, I will help thee; yea; I will uphold thee
with the right hand of my righteousness."*
—ISAIAH 41:10

To all that have lost a loved one, you know what
grief is. The rest of you may not know the
depths of this pain but there will come a day that
you will be required to go through this also. Only
through my faith in the Lord Jesus Christ did I get
through a day. The first thing I did when my eyes
opened each morning was think of my three sons,
desiring to pray for them as I had done every day of
their life. All of a sudden there was that realization

that one was gone. I would cry and even call out loud to God, "Ky where are you? Why did you do this?" The heartache and pain in the pit of my stomach were almost unbearable. When I would go out in public, I would see someone that looked like him and I would want to go running to him. I could hear his voice. I could hear his car drive up. I could hear the front door open and know he was walking up the stairs. Oh my precious son, how I hurt!

Shay was living in Orlando, Fl. and Chad and his family were living in Pensacola, Fl. Chad, Brenda, their two month old little boy and Shay stayed with us two weeks following the funeral. When they returned to their homes, their planes left Memphis 5 minutes apart. I had held together pretty well so they wouldn't see me cry but when they turned to go to the plane, I thought I would die. George and I held on to each other as we walked, crying to the car.

Just to have something else to think about, George wanted to stop at a bearing shop to get some bearings for our nephew Phillip's go-cart. As he went in, I looked up to the most beautiful, clear, blue sky I had ever seen. With a stomach-wrenching cry, I said, "God if my baby is in the arms of Jesus, show me a bird". I saw this flicker way up in the sky and I thought it was an airplane. To my total amazement, here comes a bird, straight at my window and as I gazed at that bird, there came one from the left and one from the right and then all three birds flew up into the beautiful sky. I know this is hard for some of you to believe but it happened and it gave me a tremendous peace. When George came out of the shop, I shared what had happened. He did not doubt it for one minute. As I have shared this with friends it always brings tears. When I begin to doubt where my child is, I remember that moment when God sent the three birds to comfort this mother.

Shay moved home soon after Ky's death. It was such a blessing to have him with me but now I could see the grief in his eyes and as well as those of his father. We were hurting! It would not go away for any of us. It was there and it was real. I wanted to comfort my boys and my husband and I didn't know how.

I realized one day how I was pushing my loved ones away. I didn't understand myself. Then Shay said to me, "Mom I know what you are doing, if you push us away then if something happens to one of us, it won't hurt so badly." Oh no, I didn't want that. I didn't want to hurt my family. They were hurting just like me over our loss. Finally we came to a point that we could talk about Ky. We could talk about our feelings. My sons and husband realized we needed to talk to each other and share what we were feeling.

I remember the night that I realized my husband and I were just sitting and staring out in space or at the television, not saying a word to each other. I realized that this terrible hurt was tearing us apart as a couple. I knew I could not bear to lose my husband. I said, "honey you have to talk to me". He began to share his feelings with me; he had not been doing so because he did not want me to hurt more. He was a runner and he told me that as he ran by the spot where Ky died, he talked to him. He knew Ky would not be talking back to him but he felt better by expressing his feelings in this way. Then I knew that my husband was as torn to pieces as I was. I knew I must reach out to him and to love him through his pain. I wasn't the only one hurting.

Knowing I did not want to push anyone of my loved ones out of my life, I began to share my hurts with them and they did with me. I cannot say if this helped the pain or not but it kept us close as a family. It took more than a year for us to be able to say, "I remember being here with Ky". Everywhere we looked we could think of a time that he had been there with us. It is still very hard to get picture albums out of the closet and go through the pictures of vacations and special occasions that we shared as a family.

Through this tragedy, I turned to God like never before. It seemed that after the funeral, my friends did not know what to say to us. I felt so alone in my pain. Only a couple of friends even came to see us. The church family did not know what to do for us, so Ky was not mentioned nor was our grief. If I could say anything to church leadership it would be to have an ongoing support group ministry for the grieving. George and I needed help so we turned to a support group outside our church family. It was not Christ centered and the people there did not know what to say to us either. They had become friends over a period of meeting together for three years. They were at the point they could laugh and enjoy the meeting. They just rehashed the past three years every week. I left as empty as I was when I came.

I knew then that all I needed was God. I got into His word as soon as I ate my breakfast every day. Sometimes I would spend an entire day just reading the Bible and talking to Him. It got to the point that I could feel his presence like he was sitting in the room with me. I loved it! I felt comforted. My God was so real to me. I had often given my testimony at churches and I was asked to share my testimony at the Naval Air Station. I had spoken there before but this time I said no. Months later I was asked again and I felt the Lord was telling me to share about Ky. I did! Because I shared my pain, I had many people come to me and share their grief. God has used my testimony in ways that I never thought possible. If you are grieving today, don't worry about people meeting the emptiness that you feel, turn to our Lord Jesus for the only real comfort available. He will never leave you nor forsake you. I know that he counted every tear that I shed and will continue to shed. May God bless you, as He has my precious family and me, as you go through this day, regardless of how you are hurting.

I would like to encourage young people to talk to their parents or a school counselor when they feel bad. It could save you from a lot of pain. It is difficult for the ones that love you to know if you are depressed or just having a tough time. As a former teacher, I had many students come to me and tell me things they did not want to share with a parent. Find a sensitive caring teacher and talk. They love you.

Parents listen to your children. Ask them about their interests and get them involved in something they enjoy doing. If there isn't anything for young people to do in your community, I suggest you start something. Sitting in front of the television set is not an activity and should not be a baby sitter for a parent. Children would much rather have their parents doing things with them.

Children need a happy environment. They need parents that love them and respect their thoughts. Our children need and desire discipline. Rules are to be made by the parent and to be obeyed by the children. If rules are broken then there should be a consequence. All children should have parents that they can respect. You as a parent need to live in such a way that you deserve respect. My mother taught me to respect her by the life she led. She taught me to honor my elders and to love my Lord Jesus. Bible verses come in handy as a teaching tool when dealing with your children. You have to love them through their heartaches and disappointments. Remember they live in a world that is totally different from the one you grew up in. There are so many temptations in their world that you and I did not have to deal with. Teach them to respect themselves and not follow the lead of the ones going in the wrong direction. If you have done your parenting correctly, children will know what is wrong and what is right. The leaders that go in the right direction are the winners in life.

"I will praise Thee, O Lord, with my whole heart; I will tell all Thy marvelous works"

—PSALMS 9:1

Ky

Ky was my first child, sweet and wonderful
He was the one who wanted everything
    perfect
His hair, his clothes, his room and his family
A finer boy you would never see
As a little boy he was a wonder
Smart in school and was no trouble
He was loved deeply by his brothers
His dad and especially his mother
Away to college he went one day
It broke my heart needless to say
Suddenly he drastically changed
No one could understand why he did these
    things
To the doctor we went then the heartache
    came
Bipolar was a new name
These things we do not understand
Why did our child have to suffer this disease?
His medication he would not take
His life he did, Oh what a mistake!

CHAPTER ELEVEN

The Peace Came

"From the rising to the sun unto the going down of the same the Lord's name is to be praised."

—PSALMS 113:3

I praise God today as he has brought me through the valleys. I can thank Him for the valleys that he has allowed me to encounter in my life. Valleys are not easy but through them he has grown me. I have a long way to go to be like Jesus but I have never desired that more than I do at this point of my life. Mountaintops are great and I feel like I could rule the world when I am there but thank God I do not stay there. I have found that when everything is going great and I feel great, that is when Satan attacks and I get to thinking I can do everything or anything on my own. That is when I do not lean on Jesus like I should. I do not hunger for his word, nor do I pray as often. Human nature is a complex thing and I beg for His presence in my life when I need Him.

God did not bless me with a talent for writing. I barely passed my college English. After a serious throat surgery I asked God to give me something to do that would bless Him. A few days after that prayer, I woke up with poems in my head. I sat down at my computer and began to write them down. Thus far I have published three little books of poetry that I give away as a ministry for my Lord. God has blessed those little books in a might way. So many people have called, written and told me in person of the blessings they have received from reading my thoughts. God certainly has a sense of humor, when he can have one of his children like me to write poetry because I do not like poetry.

The sharing of my grief and the opportunity to write it in the form of prose was therapy for me. All my feelings came pouring out. Many people who have lost a child or a loved one have told me how much they enjoyed reading about my pain and then knowing that they were not alone in their own pain.

God has given me peace through my heartache and grief. There was a point in all of this where I thought I would never be at peace. The peace came and I am so thankful for my Lord Jesus and His ever presence in my life. The day I turned my thoughts to Christ and took them off myself, was the day I realized peace had entered in. God has guided my path through it all. May God bless you as He guides you through your valleys.

"Give, and it shall be given unto you; Good Measure, Pressed Down, and Shaken Together, and running over."

—LUKE 6:38

Thank You

Thank you God for guiding my path
Through the valley where you held my hand
The mountain tops that you tugged on me to
   climb
My parents that were given to me by your
   divine order
For my children that you sent to me in your
   timing
I praise you for my salvation

The mind that you gave me to understand the
  Old Rugged Cross
For your presence in my life today
Thank you Lord for your patience with a sin-
  ner such as I
The love that you have shown through the
  wrong paths that I chose
The many friends that you sent into my life to
  love
Thank you for the guidance you will give me
  tomorrow
For the forgiveness that you have given me
  today
Continue to guide my path dear Lord
The path that seems so uncertain to me
You know where I am going and you know
  where I have been
Thank you for listening to my prayers
Some of which were just whining and begging
  from me
Thank you

Printed in the United States
41299LVS00002B/127-228